TESTED AND TRIED

Accessing the Power of Prayer and Abundant Grace

Sanola Rose Lawrence

TESTED AND TRIED. Copyright © 2025. Sanola Rose Lawrence. All Rights Reserved.

Printed in the United States of America.

No portion of this book may be reproduced, stored in a retrieval system, or transmitted in any form or by any means, except for brief quotations in printed reviews, without the prior written permission of DayeLight Publishers or Sanola Rose Lawrence.

ISBN: 978-1-966723-35-6 (paperback)

Cover designed by Lamoy Campbell

Scripture quotations marked "KJV" are taken from the Holy Bible, King James Version (Public Domain).

DEDICATION

This book is dedicated to my readers who have found themselves in situations that tested their faith and caused them to question the very existence of God.

This is your personal reminder that you are not alone. You are never alone. Many of us stand with you as some of those who have been tested and tried, and who have, through it all, accessed the power of prayer and have been recipients of His abundant grace.

ACKNOWLEDGEMENTS

I would like to express my deepest gratitude to some very important individuals who guided me along the journey of a thousand steps to this moment of writing this book.

Special thanks to my family, particularly my parents, sisters, brothers, and other extended family members, for their support throughout this journey of faith. The story of each is unique but has, in one way or another, inspired me and, on many occasions, lifted my faith when it wavered.

To my darling husband, for his unwavering support and his constant, countless reminders that giving up was not an option.

Heartfelt thanks to my church family, The Clover Hill Seventh Day Adventist, whose love and prayers have proven to be a tower of strength over the years, and who have helped me numerous times unlock the power of prayer.

I would also like to express my appreciation to my book and writing coach, Crystal Daye of DayeLight Publishers, who provided invaluable insight and guidance throughout the journey. She helped make this dream a reality by encouraging me to push beyond my comfort zone and step out of it.

Most importantly, I want to say thanks to the Almighty for wisdom, health, strength, and the inspiration so that others can be motivated, inspired, and impacted by my writing.

TABLE OF CONTENTS

Dedication iii
Acknowledgements v
Introduction 9
Chapter 1: What Is Grace? 11
Chapter 2: A Family of Grace 17
Chapter 3: The Distress Signal 29
Chapter 4: God Smiled on Me 35
Chapter 5: And Then He Frowned, Or Did He? 47
Chapter 6: Your Spare Tyre? Or Your Engine? 61
Chapter 7: The D-Obstacles 65
Chapter 8: White Collar Criminal 81
Chapter 9: Breaking Chains 87
Chapter 10: Experiencing Transformation 95
Poems From the Author 103
About the Author 107

INTRODUCTION

Have you ever felt like you hit rock bottom? Like that feeling of hopelessness that causes you to feel uncertain if your prayers are even being answered? Have you ever felt like you are living the reality of the story of Job in the Bible? Like everything that could go wrong has gone wrong?

If your answer to any of those questions above is yes, then you have picked up the right book. I have been in similar positions at some point in my life, and I had to learn to access the power of prayer. Now, I am a living testimony of that very same power. In fact, it was during my period of being tested and tried that I truly learned to pray. Not only to pray but to understand His voice, because His voice truly makes a difference.

You, too, can experience the power of prayer in your life. You, too, can break the chains that seem to hold you captive. You, too, can be transformed and renewed.

Activate the power of prayer today.

CHAPTER 1

WHAT IS GRACE?

Have you ever been tested and tried? Or more specifically, has your faith ever been tested and tried? Well, if you have ever been in those trying situations where your faith in Christ was truly tested and you felt overwhelmed, feeling like you were going under, you are not alone. There are many people around the world who can identify with you and echo similar, if not identical, sentiments. Some of you can attest to being tested and tried to the point where you could not see beyond your current position at that very moment in time. It may have felt like there was no tomorrow. Even time may have stood still, and the world seemed to have stopped its rotation. But be reminded that God's grace is sufficient for you.

If you ask any Bible-believing Christian what grace is, then they will quote or describe it as the "unmerited favour of God." They may further explain that it is unmerited in the sense that it is something or a favour that we do not deserve, yet He gives us anyway. What an awesome God!

God's grace is evident in the scriptures, right across the entire sixty-six books of the Bible, both in the Old and New Testaments.

If we examine Genesis 6:5-7, we will see how the wickedness of humanity was so great on the earth that it grieved God. Let us look at the text as cited below from the King James Version Bible:

> **And God saw that the wickedness of man was great in the earth, and that every imagination of the thoughts of his heart was only evil continually. And it repented the LORD that he had made man on the earth, and it grieved him at his heart. And the LORD said, I will destroy man whom I have created from the face of the earth; both man, and beast, and the creeping thing, and the fowls of the air; for it repenteth me that I have made them. (KJV).**

Verse 6 says it repented the Lord that He had made man. A definition of repent, as seen in the King James Bible Dictionary, is to feel pain, sorrow, or regret for something done or spoken. Now, if we contextualize the word "regret" as seen in the text, we will understand that God was grieved. He felt deep pain or sorrow based on what was taking place on the earth. Man, and the extent of their sin, caused Him great sorrow.

Tested and Tried

But amidst all that was happening, verse 8 speaks to the fact that Noah found grace in the eyes of the Lord. Noah received "unmerited favour." No matter your situation or circumstance, you too, like Noah, can receive grace. Our gracious God will not hesitate to extend His arms of mercy towards you. It is within His power to punish, yet He stands ready to freely pardon, to offer compassion and forgiveness. But, condition applies. This condition is found in 1 John 1:9:

> **If we confess our sins, he is faithful and just to forgive us our sins, and to cleanse us from all unrighteousness. (KJV).**

He knows what we have done. He knows where we have been. In fact, He knows even the very thoughts we have right now about plans that do not align with His will. Yet in His infinite wisdom and His abundant and unlimited grace, He gives us the freedom of choice. He is a loving God, one who loves us in spite of our shortcomings.

Growing up as a child in St. Elizabeth with my aunt, her husband, and their kids—who I affectionately refer to as my second set of parents and siblings—I received unmerited favors from my uncle-in-law (whom I called Daddy). He was always a mediator between me and my aunt. I can recall one day, I went into the refrigerator and took out the platter that had a sumptuous golden brown stewed fish. I tasted it and found it so delicious that I ended up eating an entire side. I placed it back so the uneaten side was turned up, and no one knew the difference. It was not until my aunt (mama) was ready to reheat it and share it for her husband that she recognized it was only half of a fish. She asked among us to find out who did it. I thought that if I confessed, then I would be spared from punishment. So I did. She reached for the rod of correction, and he (daddy) stepped in, made a joke of the situation, and rescued me from being spanked. Looking back now as an adult, I dare say I know I deserved the rod, but grace was extended.

Fortunately, Christ tells us that if we confess, He is faithful and just to forgive us. He promised not only to forgive us but to cleanse us from all the filthiness of sin. But in order for us to be recipients of this forgiveness and cleansing, we have to confess everything to Him. We have to come "clean" with Him about all our wrongdoings. This confession will ultimately lead to receiving God's grace and repentance. Repentance here means turning away from sin and thereby aligning ourselves with His will for our lives.

This will not always be as easy as we would expect it to be. Repentance is a process and, quite frankly, not one that is achieved overnight. This has to be taken in stages. In my research, I came across an article that showed repentance could be conceptualized in four major steps:

- **Recognition** – At this stage, the individual recognizes that a change is needed. He/she recognizes that they need God's intervention and His grace, His unmerited favor in their lives, however undeserving.

- **Remorse** - This is the stage where one feels the pangs of regret and guilt. Now, one cannot allow oneself to be stuck at this stage. It is good to recognize that there is a problem, and it is even better when that is followed by remorse, or what we may call regret. I believe it is imperative at this level to become more engaged in forging a connection with Christ and to let Him provide solutions to whatever you are facing. Because, frankly, you cannot do it on your own. You have to now learn how to activate the power that can be unleashed through prayer and lay claim to God's abundant grace and the blessings that He has reserved just for you.

- **Resolution** - We are now at the point where we make a firm decision to accept the corrective measures that were laid down. And that is if, while we were praying, we were not just busy talking to our Creator, but actively communicating. In effective communication, the channel is open both ways. So, we speak to Him and we also take the time to listen to what He has to say.

- **Reform** – At this stage, your life is changed for the better, and the grace of God is evident.

You can be a recipient of His abundant grace today. How? Christ remains faithful and forgiving, even when we are undeserving. Your response to such grace should be simple. Repent and accept the outpouring of His love, His unmerited favour. No matter who you are or how you feel, just let go and let God.

CHAPTER 2

A FAMILY OF GRACE

A few years ago, I shared the story of how my family, like Noah, found grace in the eyes of the Lord. My aim was to express the goodness of God towards us and encourage others to trust Him because He is faithful and just. However, there are a few people who chose to see the opposite. In fact, some people commented that it must have been something we did wrong and that there is a "curse" on the family. Now, might I add that some of these comments came from people I least expected. This brought the Job story to the forefront of my mind. He was ridiculed by the very friends he expected to bring him words of comfort as he faced his crucible. But as for us, still we pressed on, resolute in our relationship with the King of heaven. I will share a few of our "grace-filled" stories with you.

On May 4, 2010, my eldest sister was on her way from evening classes when the vehicle she was travelling in crashed into a parked truck. She was the front passenger and sustained multiple injuries. We got numerous calls that night that left us feeling weak in the knees. Why? We were told by some that she died on the spot, some said she was still alive when she left the scene, but due to her condition, she won't make it. We were paralyzed by fear.

But let me hasten to add that my family has a strong spiritual legacy stemming from our paternal grandparents. Additionally, we had family members and friends who were interceding in prayer groups all over, both locally and internationally. From various denominations, the Christian community was praying. Suffice it to say, after having splinters in one of her eyes, a cracked pelvic bone, spinal injury, damaged neck, and a left arm that was broken multiple places, even the doctors saw a hopeless situation. With apologetic tones, they informed her that she would never walk again.

To this day, her eyes light up when she shares her story of how she stopped the doctor in his tracks and told him about the God she serves. After a few months of being hospitalized, with plates and screws in her left arm, her neck in a neck support brace, and legs that forgot how to move, she came home. The journey of learning to walk again was tedious, but by the grace of God, she became a living testimony of grace. Today, she is still a teacher by profession, an MC extraordinaire, an exceptional wife, mother, daughter, sister, and friend.

She held on to the hope expressed in Romans 8:18. The Apostle Paul wrote: **"For I reckon that the sufferings of this present time are not worthy to be compared with the glory which shall be revealed in us." (KJV).**

Tested and Tried

Let us take a moment to highlight the word "suffering." As Christians, we will have our tests and trials. But we look forward in hope, knowing that it is just for the "present time." Whenever we have individuals close to us going through challenging times, we often like to remind them that "this too shall pass."

As for me, sometimes I find it easy to say comforting words to others, but when I am the one sitting the exam of tests and trials, those same words or thoughts are not so easy to comprehend. But that is what it really is: "just for a moment." We may not know when it will pass, but we can rest assured that it will. We may not even know when things will change, but God is working it out for your good.

Let me hasten to tell you that my sister's story did not end there. She, along with her husband and daughter, would see another test coming when she gave birth to her son in June 2014. He is what we would call our "miracle boy." He was born very sick.

He had bleeding on the brain, eye problems; they said he was deaf, his left lung had collapsed, and the other was barely holding out. He lived at the hospital for months following his birth, and for the first few years of his life, his hospital visits were so frequent that we lost count.

Again, the prayer warriors in the family and elsewhere rallied to the cause. All this while her daughter was preparing for high school. She, too, was not taking it well, and although she was but a child, she was showing signs of stress, including headaches and tension in the back of her neck. I can recall, at one point, my sister and her husband had to be called in because the doctors had given up hope. When they got there, he was pronounced dead. My sister would tell you that she and her husband stood there and prayed, and the machine that was attached to him surged with signs of life. The doctors were amazed. But as she told them, it had nothing to do with them. It was God at work. Today, that same miracle boy is a little prayer warrior and preacher of the word.

It is truly amazing what prayer can do. Never underestimate the power of prayer. A section of James 5:16 states that the effectual fervent prayer of a righteous man availeth much. So, as long as you go to God with all honesty and sincerity and you seek to live a life that is pleasing to Him, then your prayer will be effective. You will see the desired result in your life and in the lives of those you are interceding for.

What if you are not living your life in a way that is pleasing to God? Well, we have all sinned and come short of the glory of God, but His grace is boundless, and He freely offers us forgiveness and redemption. His grace is sufficient to pardon and strengthen us in our weakest moments and be our light in our darkest seasons.

Tested and Tried

In retrospect, God's grace carried us to where we are today. Were it not for grace, we would not have survived many situations that the devil meant for evil. But it is truly amazing what prayer, trust, and faith in God can do.

My younger sister has had numerous "grace-filled" incidents as well. The most irrefutable one is when she went into the hospital for surgery, and during the process, her heart stopped for a longer period than it should have. We would not have been privy to this had the doctors not explained it to our mother at the end of the procedure. From what they had seen, they had witnessed a miracle and encouraged her to keep trusting in God. Their exact words were "Your daughter died and came back to life." Might I add that, as far as I know, this doctor may not have been a Christian, but there he was, encouraging others to remain faithful to God. That is the power of the God we serve. We rejoice continually because of His goodness towards us.

> **O give thanks unto the LORD, for he is good: for his mercy endureth for ever. (Psalm 107:1 – KJV).**

If comprehensive details were to be given for each family member, this book would be a large and hefty volume. However, let us delve deeper into more "grace-filled" moments in the lives of my family members.

My eldest brother has had his fair share of ups and downs; his fair share of trials. He has weathered many storms that were meant to break him, but he stands as an inspiration to many. Personally, I admire his love for God and the relationship that he has with Him. I have witnessed the Lord getting him out of many traps laid by the enemy and saving His life on many occasions. Sure, he is not perfect, and neither will he tell you otherwise, but through it all, he is a living testimony that "Grace will always be greater than sin."

Another story that is worth being repeated is one in which another one of my brothers was almost electrocuted by lightning one day as he went out to give assistance to a friend. He was struck by lightning, which left his tongue scorched/burnt, and he would tell you that his hand was transformed into a black "object." We use the term "object" because, as he said, had his hand not been on his body, he may not have recognized it. He would have also told you that if it had not been for God on his side, he would not have lived to tell the tale. But we know that according to Psalm 34:7, **"The angel of the LORD encampeth round about them that fear him, and delivereth them." (KJV).**

His life was spared because he has a purpose. God was not and is still not through with him.

As we continue through the corridors of time, I can also vividly recall hearing my father recounting the story of

Tested and Tried

my youngest brother, who was almost hit by a car. As I recall the story, he always took care of his animals as a young lad, which he still does to this day. He was holding the rope of one of his goats when a car seemed to have come out of nowhere. As the older siblings and my parents would say, they expected to see him lying in the road, but he escaped unharmed, and the "scapegoat" was lying where he should have and could have been. Was it a mere chance of luck? Absolutely not. God stepped in right on time because that is exactly who He is—an on-time God.

My mother, our prayer warrior, has suffered five strokes to date, and through it all, she remains faithful to the God she serves and remains constant in prayer. To this day, she can move around without the assistance of others. I like to refer to her as a living testimony of God's grace. Many people that we have known over our lifetime, as well as those we have heard about, did not live to tell the tale after one stroke or even two. But she always bounces back after therapy and is there praying with and for others who are faced with their share of tests and trials. Have you ever heard the term, "Not easily broken?" Well, that is my mother. Not in her own strength or by her own strength, but because of grace and mercy and the power of prayer.

If our parents taught us nothing else, they taught us how to rely on God, and they instilled in us the power of prayer. That is one of the greatest legacies we could ever receive from them. In reality, and in all honesty, some of us may not have embraced or fully understood it in our younger days. However, as the years progressed and adulthood took its stand, we became more appreciative of the legacy they passed on to us.

They were guided by Proverbs 22:6, **"Train up a child in the way he should go: and when he is old, he will not depart from it." (KJV).**

As mentioned earlier, some persons theorized that there was a curse on the family. Why? In that same year, 2010, when my sister had her accident, we would see another attack on our family. When my older sister was finally discharged from the hospital and was on her way home, my younger sister was on her way to the very same hospital, as she had been in an accident that day.

She was on her way home from school (she was in High School at the time) when the taxi she was traveling in had an accident. She was taken to the hospital for them to rotate the shoulder back in place, as it had been dislocated. It was the year that my brother was almost electrocuted, my mom suffered another stroke, my other brother almost lost a finger (while cutting boards, the machine he was using cut off one of his fingers and he held it together until he got medical attention; the piece he was holding was stitched back in place), and my father had injured his leg and had to be home for a few days from work.

Tested and Tried

I was just amazed at how the Lord came through for each family member, and we stayed in praise and thanksgiving mode. But for some of the others looking on, it was assumed that we must have been involved in some form of wrongdoing, and we were paying the penalty. And yes, some of these individuals were those from whom we expected quite the opposite. Amidst all the hurtful comments, was I disheartened? I sure was, but not for reasons they would have thought. In a rather odd way, I was wondering why, if my sins were that grave, I was not tested like the others. This may seem a bit anomalous to some, but allow me to explain.

On numerous occasions, I have been privy to discussions indicating that there are individuals who don't cause the devil to panic. Why? There are some people with whom he feels comfortable. When he knows he has you in his grasp, he often just lets you be, diverting his attention and energy to pursuing those who threaten his existence because they seek a deeper, more meaningful relationship with Christ.

(By means of introspection, ask yourself, "Is the devil comfortable with me?")

So, considering those memories, I was left wondering why he was leaving me alone. I was somehow reminded that everyone faces different seasons in their lives, and at different times. So, I had to embrace the reality that this was not my season. As the years progressed, there was a paradigm shift as I too would have my fair share of trials.

A few years ago, on January 10, 2021, I was at home when my eldest brother returned my car. We agreed that I would take him back to his bus stop so he could get a taxi home, or I would just take him home. Before we left, he was there singing his heart out as usual (he is an excellent singer by the way), and I was there explaining something from the Bible to a close friend of mine who was staying with me for a few months. She wasn't a Christian and wanted to understand more about some scriptures, and I know the devil was not pleased with any of us.

When we left, I drove to the gate and stopped, waiting for the car coming our way to pass by so I could head onto the main road. However, instead of passing by, the car headed straight at us. I was around the wheels, my brother in the passenger seat, and my friend in the back; all we could do was brace for the impact. We were shaken, oh yes, we were. When we stepped out of the car and started making calls, I saw a missed call from my dad. I returned his call, and before hearing about the accident, he asked if I was okay because he was sitting down and just felt a strong urge to pray for his children, especially for me. He said he obeyed, knelt down, and was interceding for his children.

Now do you understand the power of prayer?

Tested and Tried

I am confident of this fact because, had it not been for him praying in that moment, I am sure the story would have ended differently for us that evening.

Many times, we are saved from certain situations, not because of our own merits but because we have friends and family members interceding on our behalf. They are mentioning our names to God, seeking intervention in situations that are beyond our control. Not only that, but seeking guidance and pleading for us lest we go astray, or even praying for grace and mercy to surround us when we do go astray.

CHAPTER 3

THE DISTRESS SIGNAL

According to an AI overview definition on Google, a distress signal is a method used to alert others—such as a rescue team, that you are in a dangerous—immediate situation and in need of assistance. Likewise, many times in our lives when we are faced with hopeless situations, we can call on others to intercede on our behalf.

We are encouraged in Galatians 6:2 to **"Bear ye one another's burdens and so fulfil the law of Christ." (KJV).** We often repeat this text and see it in its simplicity. But when we ponder the same text, bearing another's burden means a part of that individual's burden will now rest on you. So inevitably, you will end up sharing the load so the other person will have a lesser 'weight' to carry.

Let me share an example that may help to give us a visual image of what I am saying. About a month before compiling this book, our church was engaged in construction as we sought to expand our building. Now, everyone wanted to play a part in this, and for each planned workday (we met on some scheduled days to do work at the church), even the ladies were busy doing what they could to help.

On one particular day, they asked everyone to go a few chains away from the church to collect some boards. When we got to the location, some of us ladies, like myself, took one look at the boards and deemed it a rather daunting task, especially for us. I saw it as a man's job and felt as if I was biting off more than I could chew; it was more than I could manage.

I tried lifting one alone, but I couldn't move it, so I had to put it back down. Someone suggested that we try holding one end and allow someone else to hold the other. We tried it that way, and the same board that was so heavy suddenly felt lighter. Pretty soon, we traversed the distance between the church and that area multiple times. Interestingly, on our last trip, some of us returned empty-handed because we were so eager to carry those boards that we didn't realize the stockpile had dwindled until there was none left.

So, at first, the task seemed impossible, and the burden too much to bear alone. But as soon as the burden was shared, the load became lighter. Even though the board was still the same size and weight, it was now manageable just because it was shared.

Now let us get back to Galatians 6:2. Bearing one another's burden may not be as literal as in the case of transporting the boards, but rather by interceding for one another—trying to understand what the other person is going through and standing in the gap for that individual, and displaying more empathy rather than mere sympathy.

As a matter of fact, Christ sees what you are going through. He is touched with the feelings of our infirmities (see Hebrews 4:15). He is the real burden bearer. So even if or when you are too weak to call on others for help, He will send help when you least expect it, and often from unexpected sources. There may be times when someone just comes up to you and randomly asks if you are doing okay. Your response may be a masked one, for example, "Yes, I am fine. Why do you ask?" But they may have seen your distress signal, even though you aren't even cognizant of sending one out.

It may sometimes leave you wondering whether someone whom you had confided in had betrayed your trust. I have had these very same feelings. You may just be perplexed by the very thought that someone is offering you solace in a moment that you never expected or even asked for.

Well, my friend, guess what? That is just a distress signal being answered. This is irrefutable evidence that God loves you. He cares for you. Answering your distress signals in various ways shows that He is looking out for you.

Sanola Rose Lawrence

TESTS VERSUS TESTIMONIES

Who do you know that has never been tested? Absolutely no one. The reality is that we have all been tested in one way or another. We have found ourselves in situations that pushed us to even question our very faith and beliefs. In fact, sometimes when our backs are against the wall, we may even question the very existence of God.

We often see our trials as punishment and may feel as if we have been forsaken and forgotten by the one we call "Abba."

However, our tests and trials are not meant to break us but to give birth to our testimonies. Interestingly, even though I have never borne children of my own, based on experiences shared by others, the birthing process is a painful one. Some people will tell you about their ordeal, which went on for hours and was probably worse than they could have ever imagined. But after the pain has passed, there is the joy and fulfilment of holding that newborn baby. So just imagine the beauty that is revealed when you have been through the painful process of being tested and stand on the other side of that test, having given birth to your testimony?

We are often reminded through various mediums that if there is no test, there will be no testimony. If we reflect on our school days, we will recall that after being exposed to the content of a particular course, we are tested. The

Tested and Tried

tests are typically designed to inform the teacher about what you have grasped, to identify your weak areas, and to determine whether there is anything the teacher or facilitator needs to reinforce. Often, the teacher will provide insight into the test's focus, but you may not know how the questions will be structured.

Likewise, in this school of life, there are many lessons being taught daily. As we go through the lessons, we are often tested to see where we are along the journey. There are times when we are tested to teach us how to be patient. At other times, we are tested in ways that drive us to our knees and cause us to learn how to rely solely on Christ and trust Him wholeheartedly. But be sure that whatever the test, there is a testimony loading. He hears the cries of your heart, and deliverance is on the way. Just trust and believe. Keep sending out your distress signals, and remember that help is on the way. As mentioned before, distress signals are sent out involuntarily, even when we are not aware of sending any such signal.

Always remember His promise in Psalm 34:17, **"The righteous cry, and the Lord heareth, and delivereth them out of all their troubles." (KJV).**

> **Many are the afflictions of the righteous: but the Lord delivereth him out of them all. (Psalm 34:19 – KJV).**

Affliction is termed as a *"state of pain, distress, grief, or misery; a cause of mental or bodily pain, as sickness, loss, calamity, or persecution."* However, the Bible constantly reminds us that we can rest assured because there is hope even in the midst of our suffering. One of the reasons suffering persists is that it is one of God's tools for humility.

Suffering reminds us that we are finite humans, meaning we have a limited time span and a physical body with limitations. But through these same sufferings, we are also reminded that there is an infinite God, with limitless possibilities and capabilities. His grace is bigger than any affliction or circumstance that you have faced or that you will ever face.

Again, His grace is sufficient for you.

CHAPTER 4

GOD SMILED ON ME

For years, I was prayerful and hopeful that the good Lord would smile on me and grant me a family of my own. I was beginning to feel hopeless and even thought that marriage and family were not for everyone, definitely not for me.

I had been in relationships before where I thought that this was it, and then, for one reason or another, it didn't work out. I began to be more specific in my prayers, and God showed me my best friend of over ten years at the time. I had so many excuses, to the point where I reminded God that he was not a Christian. Still, the voice spoke. We decided to step into uncharted waters and give the relationship a try. A few months later, he began tuning in to online programs and started visiting church. One day, he made his decision and informed me that he wanted to surrender to the Lord in baptism. He had his baptism date set for Sunday, March 13, 2022, contacted the pastor of our church, and took his bold step.

A few months later, on May 22nd, we walked down the aisle and pledged our love for each other. For me, this was God's grace at work in my life. Why? He saw it fit to bless me with a wonderful husband at a time when I had all but given up on love and marriage.

In essence, this is a constant reminder that God's timing is way different from man's timing. He may not come when you want Him, but rest assured that He is always on time.

You may be praying for a breakthrough and on the verge of giving up, feeling as if God does not know your name or address (and yes, I have heard this phrase used by more than one individual). However, that may be because you are operating from your clock. It is therefore imperative for me to remind you to trust His timing. He is never late, never too early, but always on time.

Getting married at thirty-five was never on my schedule. That was never how it looked on the timeline that I had planned and charted out for my life. To me, the timing was way off. A part of my mind may have thought the clock was broken, because this timing was way off.

As I reflected on the scripture in Isaiah 55:8-9, I was reminded of His words that says, **"For my thoughts are not your thoughts, neither are your ways my ways, saith the Lord. For as the heavens are higher than the earth, so are my ways higher than your ways, and my thoughts than your thoughts."** (KJV).

Tested and Tried

We need to unlearn trying to work things out in our timing and trust our future to Him, because He makes all things beautiful in His time. From experience, I know it's not easy. We always speak about "all things work for our good," which I know is easier said than truly understood. In all honesty, I cannot say how He will work things out for you, but what I do know is that He knows what is best for each and every one of His children, and that includes you.

If you haven't found a companion, it might be because the time is not yet right, or perhaps God has plans for you that you must accomplish alone. It could be for a season, or it could just be your reality. Who knows?

Things are not always what they seem, and life will not always unfold as we have planned or envisioned it. That's why trust in God and trusting in God are of major importance. We have to develop a personal relationship with Him, and this is something no one can do for you. He is waiting with arms wide open, and His ears are open to your pleas. He can and He will work things out for your good.

Furthermore, we need to understand the importance of having a deep and close relationship with Him. When a father genuinely cares for his children, he will make decisions that are in their best interest. Those children, however, may not understand at first, and may even be led into rebellion.

Take my siblings and me, for example. In our younger years, we knew our father to be a strict disciplinarian, and many days we grumbled and complained. On other days, we felt like we wanted to escape all that. My sisters and I often threatened to run away whenever we were recipients of discipline or correction. My older sister, in particular, was always ready to "pack and run away." But in retrospect, we are grateful for the disciplinary measures that were taken because they shaped and molded us into the men and women we are today. As we matured, we recognized that our parents only wanted what was best for us.

Likewise, our heavenly Father allows us to be tested and tried only because He wants what is best for us. He has His ways and means of shaping and moulding us into the persons He created us to be. There is more to your story than your finite mind can comprehend. You may have lost a loved one and wonder how God could have allowed this to happen. The pain may seem unbearable, and you wonder if He even cares at all. But could it be that there is purpose in your pain? Could it be your refiner's fire?

You are loved by a loving God!

AND HE KEPT SMILING

As we sailed on into year two of marriage, things kept looking up. In 2023, we added some important items to our prayer list, one of which required a huge deposit—big enough to make this dream seem impossible. Still, we prayed on it and we prayed over it. Then came the exact period wherein the deposit was due, and we felt like we had hit rock bottom. I began cultivating and harboring negative thoughts, one of which was "This was just not going to work out."

At the end of the month, there was additional money in my account. The "extra" reflected in my salary was enough to cover the deposit without needing to take a loan. The money was a one-off payment, so yes, after making the payment, we were back to where we were financially. But God provided not only on time but also exactly what was necessary. I remember going home and sharing the news with my husband, and just the thought of how and when God came through for us was so overwhelming.

My mind pivoted back to Philippians 4:19, which states that, **"But my God shall supply all your need according to His riches in glory by Christ Jesus." (KJV).** This tells us that God will provide for our needs. His resources are endless. His storehouses are bountiful. Hence, His provision is not based on whether or not we deserve it but is solely dependent on Him and our willingness to do what it takes to unlock these resources.

His supply is always available; we just need to tap into the source. We have all had moments when we are cast in a state of chagrin, feeling hopeless as we contemplate the enormity of our needs versus our limitations. I say our limitations because, at times, our thoughts are fixed on how much we have or how much we think we have access to—not being cognizant of the fact that there is no limitation with Christ, our heavenly Father, to whom all things belong.

In 2024, a few weeks after achieving one of the main goals on our prayer list, I successfully passed an interview and was promoted to a new position. Remember the deposit that was needed, as I mentioned earlier? With that deposit, we were now homeowners, and secondly, there was the promotion.

We were once again tossed into a sea of gratitude. There was so much to be grateful for. We could clearly see where God definitely orchestrated this turn of events to ensure that monthly payments could be made without experiencing excess 'distress.' So again, the provision that God made for us was enough to secure the payments. Financially, we were not 'better off' because, technically, we had the same amount of money in our household as before that increase. However, we still had so much to be grateful for. So, considering all that, our praises and prayers increased tremendously.

We got to a point where we decided to minimize distractions as much as we could. This included giving up some movie hours and increasing our attendance at Sunday and Wednesday night meetings at church. It was through these meetings that we truly gained the strength to access the power of prayer. I was basking in the awesome feeling of being so loved by God—recognizing how much He listens, how much He cares, and how much He answers prayers.

In Luke 12:22-23, the message Christ gave to His disciples still resonates through the ages, as it is very much applicable to us today. His reminder to them was, **"Therefore I say unto you, Take no thought for your life, what ye shall eat; neither for the body, what ye shall put on. The life is more than meat, and the body is more than raiment." (KJV).**

He further implored them in subsequent verses to consider the ravens that neither sow nor reap, yet they are fed by their heavenly Father. The lilies grow, they toil not or spin, yet their beauty goes beyond even the fine arrays of King Solomon. He told them not to worry about what they would eat or drink. Why? Because He knows our needs. He knows what needs to be added unto us and exactly when it should be added. Not only does He know what is to be added, but by extension, what or even who needs to be subtracted from your life as well. All He expects of us is that we lift our faith and trust Him completely.

He wants us to keep our minds focused on heavenly things. To seek first and foremost His kingdom and all that we seek after will be added to us, as long as it is according to His will. I say *according to His will* because, at some point, we need to know how to listen to, acknowledge, and understand His voice. Sometimes, the answer will be yes. At times, it will be a definite no, and at other times, you will be told to wait and be of good courage. The answer to what you think is your dream job, dream partner, or ideal home location may be a simple 'no.' Listen to Him, learn how to recognize His voice, because His voice truly makes a difference.

Perhaps, like me, you may be praying for a child or even children, or maybe you have been praying for a breakthrough or other results in your life, and they are not forthcoming. But what if your dream does not align with God's plan for you? Does it mean that He loves you any less than His other children? The answer is a resounding *"No."*

Biblical evidence reminds us that His ways are not our ways. Again, I remind you that He knows what's best for you. I have had to remind myself so many times of this fact. This struggle really is real.

You may be seeking earthly treasures, but the treasures He has in mind to bestow upon you are of a more lasting kind.

Luke 12:34 tells us that where your treasure is, there will your heart be also. Therefore, we have to be careful about what we place our high ideals on. Keep your eyes fixed on

Christ Jesus, because He is our only hope in a world of hopelessness. We can only stay connected to Him through prayer and obedience to His Word.

Do you find yourself struggling with your prayer life? Then it is time to pray more. I am still trying to realign my time and priorities to ensure that my prayer life does not become as stagnant as a neglected pool. If a pool is left with water and neglected for a period of time, it poses a danger to your health. The water will become stagnant and contaminated. Now, this will no doubt be dangerous, as this very stagnant water will invite all manner of bacteria.

Imagine neglecting your spiritual life and allowing it to become stagnant. It will no doubt create the perfect environment for all the mold and bacteria that the devil invites into your life. You will only get rid of the mold and bacteria (sin) if you discover how to unlock the power of prayer; pray and watch God work on your behalf. He came through for me. In fact, I think He really smiled on me, and He is willing and able to do that and much more for you. He just needs your faith and obedience. He wants you to trust Him wholeheartedly. Won't you trust Him today?

OUR DAILY BREAD

As human beings, we take great care to ensure we nourish our physical bodies daily. For most of us, it is three meals per day with snacks in between. How much more ought we to feed the spiritual man? Spiritually, we should ensure that we have at least two main-course meals per day, with lots of snacks in between. We should aim to go to God in prayer before we face each day and speak to Him the last thing before bed. Those would serve as the two main meals of the day, during which we can spend some quality time with Him.

I used this analogy to explain this concept to "my" children at church while teaching their weekly lessons. I encouraged them to make a habit of giving thanks to God for waking them up to see each new day. At the end of the day, they should again give thanks for the guidance and protection they received throughout the day and ask Him to watch over them as they go to sleep. The concept of snacks between meals is like remaining constant in prayer. I encourage them to practice being thankful when they arrive safely at any destination, before eating a meal, or after any other accomplishment throughout the day. Putting these little 'snacks' into practice would greatly impact the way we see and treat our heavenly Father. Ensure that as much as you put thought into the physical food, the spiritual man is being fed as well.

Additionally, some people do not pray (believe it or not), while others admit they do not pray as much as they should. This may not be because they are neglecting God but because they are uncertain about how to pray. You are not alone. Most of us have been there. In fact, some days, while listening to others pray so eloquently, I felt so inadequate that even my prayer life suffered as a consequence.

Nevertheless, I had learnt an important lesson. We do not need words of eloquence when we talk to Him; we just need to open up to Him as to a friend. He is that friend who sticks closer than a brother—a friend who will never leave or forsake you. He will never turn His back on you.

There are seven days in one calendar week, and prayer should be a daily necessity. As we look forward to communicating with the ordinary man, we must ensure there is communication with the high King of heaven. Remember that prayer is a form of expression, so practice expressing your thoughts, feelings, and needs to the Almighty. Seek His guidance and comfort in all you do and stay connected. Might I remind you that: ***seven days make one week, but a day without prayer makes one weak.***

CHAPTER 5

AND THEN HE FROWNED, OR DID HE?

You may have read or heard of James 1:2-3, **"My brethren, count it all joy when ye fall into diverse temptations; knowing this, that the trying of your faith worketh patience." (KJV).** Verse 3 in particular holds a great degree of interest for me. It is a reminder that being tested and tried ultimately leads to strengthened faith, which helps build endurance and patience. So, in whatever situation or circumstance you may find yourself in, do not think that you are forsaken by God. Although in all practicality, some days it will seem that way. In fact, that is exactly how the devil wants us to feel. He has carefully calculated his moves to ensure that a shadow is cast on the character of Christ.

THE SHIFT

In retrospect, this lesson was not easily learnt. First, God smiled on me. Yes, things were going smoothly enough. In our daily devotion one morning, we were discussing all the major and minor victories we had experienced thus far. We expressed similar sentiments that it seemed as if we were living through the calm before the storm—

not just contemplating if things would go wrong, but wondering when.

My husband literally told me that he knows the devil was not pleased with those victories. My brother-in-law also expressed similar sentiments. Whether there is an accomplishment or someone participates in church, he always reminds us not to drop our guard and to remain prayerful, because the devil is not pleased with us. So we could just imagine the conference that he (the devil) was having, planning and plotting his next moves, dispatching legions of his demons and arming them for battle.

So through experiencing the joys of marriage, the excitement of home ownership, adjusting to new responsibilities at work, and experiencing spiritual growth, the devil attacked me physically. Within a few days of basking in the joys of the latter two that were mentioned, I became unwell. First, I experienced blurred vision for almost two weeks, and suffered silently. Silently, because outside of my immediate family members, I appeared well enough to the outside world. I could hardly see my co-workers or anything or anyone around me.

As a little back story, I struggle with Polycystic Ovarian Syndrome (PCOS). This is a hormonal condition that affects many women of reproductive age, often beginning during adolescence, and the affected person can see a fluctuation of symptoms. PCOS causes hormonal imbalances and is one of the leading causes of infertility in women. Some individuals may experience worse symptoms than others, such as excessive chest hair growth, facial hair growth, darkened skin, and thinning hairlines—you name it. Now, for most persons with such a condition, doctors often prescribe metformin, which is a medication normally prescribed for diabetic patients. This was not suggested to me however because, even though I experienced some of the symptoms like facial hair growth and irregular bleeding, it was not as bad as others were facing, based on my research and talking to other affected persons. For some people, it was these symptoms coupled with darkened skin and excessive hair growth on their chest, among others.

So when my vision grew blurry, not being a diabetic patient, the last thing on my mind was insulin resistance. My body was not using the insulin effectively, hence my blood glucose level had spiralled out of control. When I stepped into the doctor's office and he performed the glucose test, he told me he couldn't read it because the result was higher than the machine could analyze. He told me, who has never been hospitalized in my life, that I needed to go to the hospital. I also needed to see an Ophthalmologist as soon as possible to assess the damage that has obviously been done to my eyes.

During that visit to get my eyes checked, the Ophthalmologist told me to come back when my vision was a little better, so he could accurately make a prognosis. But through it all, I learnt to trust in Christ Jesus even more. I was truly not forsaken, nor did I lose hope.

As suddenly as it had appeared, the vision was cleared. Going back to the Ophthalmologist, he was amazed at what was happening with my eyes. He expected to prescribe glasses, and as he wondered what was happening, he looked me in the eyes and asked, "How are you here?" He went on to say he had seen persons whose glucose levels were still readable on the machine go into a coma or even lose their lives. The fact that this had gone above 30 mmol//L (600 mg/dL)—and based on the effects, it seemed to have been way over—was quite alarming for everyone. I capitalized on the opportunity to tell him about the God I serve. He may not come when you call Him, but rest assured that He will always be on time.

My enthusiasm, however, was a little short-lived because I had no idea that this was just the beginning. My body had a lot of healing and repairs to undergo. Over the span of a couple of months, I would experience many different feelings within my body, which were very hard to express in words. I had medical doctor visits twice weekly, and even a visit to a Naturopathic doctor. Many days, while at work, I felt as if I was at the end of the rope; the end of my days. I literally felt like there was no hope for tomorrow. I started to seek solace in the restroom, as this

Tested and Tried

was where I would make my "escape" just to fall on my knees and cry out to God to save me. I pleaded for Him to grant me the strength to see the end of the day.

I had one particular coworker who would come to my desk to check on me. Some days, I couldn't explain, and all I could say was "just pray," and she never hesitated. I had pain in my eyes and numbness in my arms, especially the right hand, which was primarily used to perform all work-related functions. Some days, that arm would not even move; I had to force it to write. How did I know the devil had launched an attack?

One Friday night, while writing a sermon, the arm went completely numb. It had one assignment at that moment: to help me prepare the word, and it failed miserably, as if it had forgotten how to write. I had to go to church in the morning and finish the sermon.

My nights were spent in restless agony. The aches and various discomforts kept me awake most nights, and the fear of not seeing the dawn kept me up during other parts of the night. I had serious pain in my eyes, weird pulsations throughout my body, especially my legs, stomach pains (the type of stomach pain that caused me to bid my husband farewell and call my older sister, telling her to please take care of him when I leave), muscle spasms, and several other complaints, some of which I didn't bother to complain about.

I remember my younger sister asking me in May 2024 about a family reunion scheduled for July of the same year. I told her I had no idea if I would still be here next week, so I couldn't think about July. I was taking things one day at a time, praying my way through, trying not to be disheartened or discouraged, and thrived on those who were responding to the distress signals—the prayer warriors who rallied to the cause.

Through it all, I was grateful, especially for the partner God had blessed me with. I like to think that God looked ahead and saw the moments I would face and made preparations for me beforehand. My husband not only prayed with me when I was awake but also prayed over me while I slept.

PRAYER CHANGES THINGS

I can attest to the power of prayer because I am living proof that prayer works. The prayers of my extended family members, my immediate family, and my church family kept me. There were days when incomprehensible and unexplainable feelings chose to take strolls through my body as easily as a walk in the park. On those days, all I could do was send out the "distress signal" via messages to my church family group and immediate family. I knew they were praying because I could feel the changes charging through my body. I could feel the peace that surpassed human understanding. As hard as it was to put my pain into words, it was equally as hard to explain the peace that permeated my mind on some days when prayer ascended on my behalf.

I remember having a day of prayer and fasting organized by one of my cousins. At the start of that day, the devil reared his ugly head. It was another of my "bad days." I could literally feel the war going on in my body. I know prayer was being offered because I could feel it. But still the war raged on. This minute, there was peace and calm, and the next, aches and pains, weird pulsations throughout my body, and a host of other feelings that cannot be put into words. However, let me hasten to tell you that God always prevails, because in the end, the victory was won.

You will be placed in situations that will rock you to the core. You will be tested and tried, but through it all, hold on to faith and the promise that He will never leave you. You will never be forsaken.

So, did God smile on me and fulfill my needs and a few of my heartfelt desires? He sure did. Did He turn His back on me? The answer is a resounding no. The God of the mountain is still God in the valley. The God who is with you as you face the calm seasons of your life is the very same God who stands with you when you face the crucibles that come.

We have often heard, whether from motivational speakers, pastors, or even songs, that all things work for our good, even when we cannot see how they could. We cannot and will not always see His purpose, but He is God—not just any God, but a good God. He has your best interests at heart. He will never leave you nor forsake you.

I have learnt to trust His heart. It is not easy. There will come a time—or many times—when the feeling of loneliness, of not even knowing your position with God, will overcome and engulf you. I can tell you, I have been there. That feeling of being abandoned is exactly what the devil wants us to feel. Submitting to this feeling brings him joy, yet it also saddens the heart of our loving and compassionate Saviour. We need not fear the one who can destroy the body, but rather fear Him who is able to destroy both body and soul in hell (see Matthew 10:28). The Bible reminds us in Deuteronomy 31:6 to, **"Be strong and of a good courage, fear not, nor be afraid of them; for the Lord thy God, He it is that doth go with thee; He will not fail thee, nor forsake thee." (KJV).**

LESSONS FROM THE JOB STORY

Whenever I find myself faced with any form of test or trial, my mind is transported back to the story of Job. Throughout the first couple of chapters, everything was the picture of perfection. In fact, as the curtains opened on the scenes of Job 1, we see the description of Job as a perfect and upright man, one who feared the Lord and eschewed evil. This fear does not mean he was fearful in his approach to his heavenly Father, but that he had deep respect and awe for the very power, presence, and existence of God. The fact that he 'eschewed' evil shows that he shunned the very appearance of evil. In other words, he hated evil and lived his life in such a way that pleased God. He was blessed with seven sons and three daughters. His substance was great. He had all his heart's desires and so much more. It was while watching these very scenes unfold that Satan presented himself to the Lord with his accusations that Job didn't respect Him for nothing. In other words, it couldn't be as simple as it seemed.

Satan ultimately got permission to touch Job's possessions but not to touch him. Job lost his possessions, but worst of all, He lost his children. Through it all, his faith did not waver. Satan went back to the meeting and got permission to "attack" Job's body. While his body deteriorated, his wife encouraged him to curse God and die, and his friends tried to insinuate that he must have wronged God in some way.

Many people who review or share this story tend to highlight Job's perfection, the losses he suffered, and dive straight into the restoration. But as for me, I take it in stages. First, there was the perfection, then there were the losses he suffered. But did he suddenly go from the loss to restoration? No. Job went through his season of grief, the season of discouragement (from family and friends), and great despair. In fact, so great was his despair that his faith wavered.

In Job 3:11, Job cursed the day he was born. He wished he had died in the womb. But through all his sufferings, he was not forsaken. In fact, restoration came in Job 42:12. We saw that the Lord blessed Job's latter end more than his beginning.

Some of my takeaways from the Job story are:

- **Seasons can change in the blink of an eye**. You can be prosperous today and that changes tomorrow. You can be healthy today and suffer an illness tomorrow.

- **It is human to feel forsaken.** You may feel forsaken and even question your very purpose or existence. But as Job did, when you bring your questions to the Father, ensure that the channel of communication is open so you will also listen to His response to you. Prayer is not a one-way street.

- **Discouragement is inevitable.** Job faced discouragement from those closest to him, including his wife and best friends. You may be faced with discouragement from those whom you least expect it—family members, friends, even your church family. Hence, it is imperative to keep your eyes and heart fixed on Jesus.

- **Your season of restoration is coming.** Job's latter end was more than his beginning. As long as we are faithful and remain constant in prayer, we will access His abundant grace.

THE CROSS AND YOUR TRIALS

Looking back at the blessings and lessons of 2024, I remain humbled and grateful. I am grateful for the blessings he bestowed, but I am also thankful for the lessons taught during my season of being "unwell." Those affiliated with me will tell you that I do not claim sickness. So they do not hear me lamenting about "sickness" but rather about when I was 'unwell.'

It was in this season that I truly learnt to pray more. That season taught me to rely on God for everything. He is able to supply my physical, spiritual, emotional, and financial needs, but on the condition that I understand His ways are not my ways, nor are His thoughts my thoughts. I no longer refused opportunities to share the word and even shared a few sermons. I like to think that He used my trials to keep me near the cross.

There is a song often sung at church, asking Jesus to keep us near the cross. But what will it take to be kept near the cross? We sing it or repeat it, but do we even understand what it means?

Yes, He will keep us near the cross, but as we have only made the request, it is up to Him to decide the means of keeping us. It may be financial tests, emotional tests, or even physical tests. You may become financially unstable, emotionally distraught, or even physically unwell. But the important thing is not to lose faith.

The devil wants to keep you from the cross, from viewing what it truly means, and from reminiscing on exactly what was accomplished at the cross. But your heavenly Father wants to keep you near the cross. Are you prepared to bear what being kept near the cross truly comes with?

Remain constant in prayer, as this is the only way you will be equipped to deal with the crucibles that will come.

When the disciples failed to cure the lunatic and bring healing, Christ Himself had to step in and heal the child, prompting the disciples to ask Him why they could not cast him (the devil) out. His response in the ensuing verses further amplifies the importance of prayer coupled with fasting, **"And Jesus said unto them, Because of your unbelief: for verily I say unto you, If ye have faith as a grain of mustard seed, ye shall say unto this mountain, Remove hence to yonder place; and it shall remove; and nothing shall be impossible unto you. Howbeit this kind goeth not out but by prayer and fasting." (Matthew 17:20-21 – KJV).**

Tested and Tried

Whenever you are faced with your tests and your trials, I implore you to always remember these important points:

- **There is purpose in your pain.** Whatever your circumstance, focus on the blessing and ensure you take note of the lesson.

- **Pray, pray, pray.** Use your tests and trials as an opportunity to go deeper in prayer. When you are faced with your crucible, practice to tell Him everything. Tell Him that, *"Lord, I do not understand what You are doing, but help me to trust You."*

- **Share your testimony.** When you have gone through your test, do not be afraid to share your story with others. Someone may be waiting to hear from you, to be empowered by you, to be strengthened by the words of your testimony.

- **Know your identity in Christ.** Know who you are and walk accordingly. You are chosen, you are royalty, claim your royal bloodline, and do not be caught up in a common lifestyle. There should be nothing common about you.

But ye are a chosen generation, a royal priesthood, an holy nation, a peculiar people; that ye should shew forth the praises of him who hath called you out of darkness into his marvellous light. (1 Peter 2:9 – KJV).

CHAPTER 6

YOUR SPARE TYRE? OR YOUR ENGINE?

A few years ago, a friend of mine was driving along one of his popular routes when he inadvertently hit a hole in the road, puncturing one of his tyres. Unfortunately, he had removed his spare tyre and his tool bag to make space in his vehicle for other things. Now, for him, there was no backup plan. No spare tyre. Luckily, he contacted a friend who was able to come to his rescue by taking a spare and the necessary tools for him.

As vehicle owners, or even if you are not the owner but are a driver, it is important to have your spare tyre and tools as a backup plan, just in case you experience a flat and need to make a change. The toolkit can come in handy, even in other cases of roadside emergencies.

Another thing I want to bring to your attention is the engines of vehicles. The engine of a car converts fuel into energy, which in turn powers the vehicle so that it can move effectively and efficiently. If the engine is faulty, then the vehicle will not be able to go anywhere. The size of the engine also contributes to how the vehicle moves. At my current place of employment, we are cognizant of the fact that the cubic capacity (cc) rating of a vehicle is an indicator of the power of the engine. The higher the cc rating, the faster and more powerful the engine of the vehicle as this correlates to the speed of the vehicle.

Now, with that said, let me ask you a very important question: Is prayer your spare tyre or is it your engine? Let us explore the analogy a bit further while you contemplate your response.

As your spare tyre, prayer will be handy. You may have your spare for weeks or even months, and you never need to use it. Similarly, you have the power of prayer, but you haven't seen the need to access it. Or that power is only activated when the need arises. You may know how to pray, but you might not see the importance of it, unless your back is against the wall.

Having prayer as your spare, you will also use it if called upon. You may be asked to pray in a church setting or even to pray on behalf of a friend, but then that is it.

We may have found ourselves in situations where we have prayed and God delivered. In some cases, we even tell Him specifically that if He gets us out of this situation this time, then we will never do anything like that again. Or better yet, we make promises. We may be experiencing sickness, and our prayer is *"Lord, I need Your healing. If You do this for me, I promise to serve You wholeheartedly."*

Tested and Tried

When He answers our prayers and we claim that healing, we suffer from "spiritual amnesia," forgetting what He did for us in the past and returning to the things we pledged never to do again. We have just used prayer as the spare tyre to get us out of that position and then stored it away until another need arises where we have to "take it out again."

On the other hand, if prayer is your engine, then you will recognize it as your power source. As the engine powers the vehicle, so will your life be powered by prayer. Prayer will not be a backup plan; instead, it will always be present in your life. Prayer will be offered, not only when a need arises but at all times. Offer prayers of thanksgiving, place your plans in the hands of the Lord, seek guidance on this bumpy road of life, and pray for every aspect of your life. You will understand how to access the power that is within your reach. Let the joy of the Lord be your strength. Be joyful and continue to lift your faith through unceasing prayer.

If, in retrospect, you realize that prayer has been your spare tyre, then it is time to make that change. Make prayer your engine today. If your life is powered by the "prayer engine," then I implore you to pray on. After all, prayer is not a spare tyre; it is the engine.

Rejoice evermore. Pray without ceasing. In every thing give thanks: for this is the will of

God in Christ Jesus concerning you. (1 Thessalonians 5:16-18 – KJV).

Cultivate an effective prayer life. Deepen your relationship with God through prayer. Be intentional and consistent, and make praying a habit. Be specific when you pray and seek to be engaged in a prayer community. This prayer community will pray with and for you as well as for others.

Ever heard the term "more prayer, more power?" Well, there you have it. Prayer can never be too much. This community often takes the form of prayer teams, which some may call prayer bands. Or it could just be a group of like-minded individuals in your phone contacts.

In addition to praying, there is also the need to immerse oneself in God's Word. For any form of direction in life, the roadmap is found in the Word of God. Studying the Word and praying without ceasing will deepen our connection with our heavenly Father.

If at any point you think you are at a crossroads and find it hard to pray or even study; if you find yourself becoming discouraged with the struggle of maintaining consistency in your prayer life, do not quit or give up. Keep pushing. As they say: Pray Until Something Happens—PUSH. Be persistent, and the Holy Spirit will be there to guide you into all truth.

CHAPTER 7

THE D-OBSTACLES

Do you find yourself dealing with Doubts and Distractions when it is time to pray? Listen, I know what this is like. In fact, the reason I brought up these two D-Obstacles is because I have been plagued by them, and at some time or another, they push up their ugly heads and seek to ruin or adversely affect my prayer life. There is also a D Obstacle called Discouragement.

Let us explore them a bit further.

DOUBT

If you consult the dictionary, one of the definitions that you will see for *doubt* is to feel uncertain about. The devil will try to cast shadows of doubt over you to discredit the power of prayer in your life. He will use past experiences to highlight reasons why praying makes no sense. He will cunningly remind you of the things you prayed for that did not come to pass. In fact, he knows that as long as he can attack your prayer life, then he will ultimately break down the barriers that have been erected for your protection. They say, "More prayer, more power," and the reverse is also true: the less you pray, the less power you have.

As for me, shadows of doubt have been cast on numerous occasions. One very dark shadow in particular is through my hormonal issues. Some days when I pray, the devils point out reasons why it makes no sense, and he uses my medical history as his weapon of casting doubt. He has blatantly told me that if I have been praying for a child and God is not answering my prayers for such a request, why do I think God will listen to me now? I had to reprogram my mind to pray to allow the Lord to have His way. This has not always been easy; in fact, it is one of the hardest things to stay in prayer, especially knowing that His ways are not our ways.

Sometimes, when I am faced with any major or minor issues, I will look to God and say, *"Lord, I cannot Your purpose see, but all is well that's done by thee"* or *"Lord, I do not understand what is happening, but increase my faith and help me to trust You more."* Sometimes my quote is paraphrased in the words of the song that says, *"all things work for my good, though sometimes I can't see how they could."*

Do not allow the devil to cloud your mind with doubt. Do not allow Him the upper hand. I have spoken to persons who are praying for their spouse/partner or even their children to surrender to God completely. While agonizing with God for a breakthrough, the devil creeps in and tries to whisper sweet, meaningless lies and casts shadows of doubt on the effectiveness of those prayers.

If you are not seeing immediate results, he will show you reasons why it is not worthwhile to continue. If you are working in the mission for Christ, helping to seek and save those who are living a life of sin, he will come to you, showing you the shortcomings of your own family, close relatives, and friends. He will blatantly tell you that you will not be successful in soul winning because you are unable to win those closest to you, those within your sphere of influence. He is very cunning. The devil knows our weak areas, and he knows when, where, and how to attack. He is often described as a roaring lion seeking to destroy you.

1 Peter 5:8 reminds us to **"Be sober, be vigilant; because your adversary the devil, as a roaring lion, walketh about, seeking whom he may devour:" (KJV).**

Now, picture a lion on the prowl, better yet, a hungry lion. He is powerful, aggressive, strong, and dangerous. The online dictionary defines *devour* as *"to swallow or eat up hungrily, voraciously, or ravenously. To consume destructively, recklessly, or wantonly."* Emphasis on the *destructively* for me. The devil does not just go on the rampage, but he is out to destroy those in his path. He is not loyal to anyone. So even if he sees that one is spending time with him and living in such a way that displeases God, he will not just sit around and wait to see what will happen. He will try to devour you, to destroy you in your sin, so you do not get a chance to make it right.

We all face various struggles with doubt, particularly concerning whether God truly answers prayers, if the power of prayer is truly accessible, or if prayer really works based on past experiences.

In order to guard and guide your minds against the negative effects of doubt, rehearse and repeat the Bible verse from **Isaiah 41:10** that says, **"Fear thou not; for I am with thee: be not dismayed; for I am thy God: I will strengthen thee; yea, I will uphold thee with the right hand of my righteousness." (KJV).**

This is really comforting and helps to relinquish the hold that doubt has over your life—knowing that Christ will always be with you, always there to uphold and strengthen you with the right hand of His righteousness. Do not allow the devil to hold you captive with having you doubt the very existence of God and the power of prayer. Fear will often sneak upon you, no doubt about that, but guess what, **"There is no fear in love; but perfect love casteth out fear: because fear hath torment. He that feareth is not made perfect in love. We love Him, because He first loved us." (1 John 4:18-19 - KJV).**

There is no record anywhere else in history or even in the Bible of any other love that is as perfect or more perfect than the love of God towards humanity. He gave His life as a ransom for the sins of the world. Oh, what a love!

Even after fear sneaks up on you and you try to conquer it, doubt will rear its ugly head and remind you that you are alone. It will remind you of all your failures and your unfulfilled dreams. Doubt will use your past to cast shadows on your future. But whatever the situation you face, remember that you are not alone. You are never alone. Your heavenly Father is with you, and additionally, whatever you are going through, there is always someone who has it worse than you. So, yes, doubts will arise; yes, fears will dismay, but let it be your aim to press forward, keep praying, and lift your faith higher.

DISTRACTIONS

The second D obstacle that wreaks havoc on one's prayer life is distraction. Distraction is anything or anyone that prevents one from concentrating on something else. In other words, anything that takes your attention away from praying. If we are not accessing the power of prayer, how then do we expect to achieve and experience God's abundant grace?

I do not know who can safely say this demonic force is not one that affects or has affected them in some way or another. I, for one, have been in situations where, during worship, I find myself looking at my phone to use the Bible app and pull the screen down to take a little peek at who messaged me. I may then proceed to respond and momentarily lose sight of what I should be reading in the first place. Hence, I try to turn off internet connections when I am in worship, but hey, this isn't always practical, as I might need to look up a word or two and find myself in a similar situation to when using the Bible app.

This may not be your reality, but how about telling yourself that you will ensure, if nothing else, to always offer a prayer of thanksgiving for the day that has ended and request his guidance for the night ahead before you sleep each night—and this is whether or not you are a church-going, Bible-believing Christian. We may even try to get it right sometimes, but inevitably, we become distracted along the way, and instead of prayer, the television puts us to sleep at night.

Additionally, the first thing we reach for in the mornings is our cell phones to scroll, instead of offering a prayer of thanksgiving for the dawn of a new day. There are many distractions that the devil will use to cause you to be disengaged or even disconnected from the power source. He wants to ensure that even if we are still plugged in, we are not connected. What does this mean?

We remain plugged in, in the sense that we attend church. We become known as faithful 'church goers' because we are seen attending church faithfully. Even those who are not regular members and may visit from time to time will tell you that they still read the Bible. So they will convince you that they are still plugged in too.

The problem ultimately does not lie with being plugged in, but with the connectivity. Have you ever plugged in your cell phone, and when you are ready to unplug it, you realize it hasn't been fully charged because you overlooked the faulty connection? Or you may have overlooked the fact that a part of the connection wasn't fully plugged in or became a little loose as soon as you let it go?

This is similar to our lives. In order for us to see God at work in our lives and experience Him for ourselves, we must ensure we are connected to Him, the true source of our strength and power. It is imperative that we not only seek to be connected but also to stay connected to that source. We can do this by minimizing our distractions and spending more time with Christ.

There are a few Bible passages that clearly tell us that He knows we will be distracted and offers us solutions beforehand:

> **2 Corinthians 11:3-4 – "But I fear, lest by any means, as the serpent beguiled Eve through his subtility, so your minds should be corrupted from the simplicity that is in Christ. For if he that cometh preacheth another Jesus, whom we have not preached, or if ye**

> receive another spirit, which ye have not received, or another gospel which ye have not accepted, ye might well bear with him." (KJV).
>
> **Hebrews 12:1-2** – "Wherefore seeing we are also compassed about by so great a cloud of witnesses, let us lay aside every weight, and the sin which doth so easily beset us, and let us run with patience the race that is set before us, Looking unto Jesus the author and finisher of our faith; who for the joy that was set before him endured the cross, despising the shame, and is set down at the right hand of the throne of God." (KJV).
>
> **1 Corinthians 10:13** – There hath no temptation taken you but such as is common to man: but God is faithful, who will not suffer you to be tempted above that ye are able; but will with the temptation also make a way to escape, that ye may be able to bear it. (KJV).

In other words, and to paraphrase, replacing the word *temptation* with *distraction*, God will not suffer you to be distracted above that ye are able, but will, with the distraction, also make a way of escape that ye will be able to avoid it.

In order to be successful in our walk with God, we will have to find ways and means of overcoming distractions. First, identify your distractor. It may be the cell phone for some, while for others it may be the television. For others, it may be relationships. In short, we chase after the things of this world instead of focusing on the weightier matters: the Word and our relationship with God, which is detrimental to our soul salvation.

Secondly, work towards eliminating or minimizing the effects of what distracts you, as much as it lies within your power to do so. In some cases, however, it is not practical to eliminate the distractions altogether, but we can control how much they control us. Take, for example, my cell phone. I cannot and will not get rid of it because that is not practical. But I can try to minimize the time spent on it and filter the things I allow myself to get caught up in.

Thirdly, be on the lookout for the subtle advances of the evil one. His aim is to destroy you in your sin. The easier you can recognize him, the more easily you will know when he is at work and be able to shun the very appearance of evil.

Fourthly, instead of getting caught up chasing after the things of this world, shift your focus to the things of God. Stay connected to the true power source through ardent study of His Word and by remaining constant in prayer.

Christ is counting on you to stand firm and be faithful to that which you are called—to be the person He created you to be. What is holding you back from having that relationship that you should? What is holding you back from praying as you ought to? For me, it was the television, and it is still a struggle. However, what helped me was being selective in the content that I watched. So we started watching more family and faith-based movies and shared them with our church group. We selected the type of content that motivated and encouraged our spiritual growth and actually had an impact on our family lives.

So yes, the movies were and still are a distraction, but with the ones we chose, I could still pray or talk about God before, during, and after the movies without feeling guilty about displeasing God with what I was watching.

DISCOURAGEMENT

Discouragement can also have a major impact on our relationship with God, in particular, your prayer life. When you are discouraged, you lack confidence and enthusiasm.

From as far back as I can remember, I used to love doing the welcome at church events. As a child, I would do the welcome for concerts, and even what we called rallies. Fast forward to my teenage years, where there was more of the same. Until one day, someone I looked up to in church told me that I should stick to other things and leave the welcome to someone else who can do a better job. Even now, I have to literally shake the thought whenever I am asked to do the welcome or anything else.

Tested and Tried

I wonder if I am good enough or if I am as good as others. My confidence wilted in light of one negative remark.

We can also become discouraged when we are no longer enthused by our prayer life. We become so busy and caught up in distractions that our focus shifts away from spending quality time with God. We are no longer intentional about meaningful prayers. In addition to distraction, some situations cause us to doubt the very existence of God. We find ourselves struggling to believe in the effectiveness of prayer due to situations we have experienced or are currently experiencing, and we cannot see or feel Him in our lives.

As mentioned before, my husband and I have been praying for a number of things. One of those things is to have a family of our own. We have fasted and prayed, and that was one of the factors that caused me to wonder for a few fleeting moments if God was really listening to my prayer. Why? At times, we have spiritual amnesia. We forget the promises that God made and the previous accounts of how He had come through for us many times before. Simply put, we "forget to remember" His goodness in our lives.

In essence, in this walk of life, we are discouraged by external factors (like other individuals and situations, past experiences) as well as internal factors of our own doing. Let us unleash the power that we have in prayer and bask in God's abundant grace, which He is waiting to bestow upon us. That power and grace can be ours as long as we are intentional about improving and maintaining our prayer lives.

KEYS TO IMPROVING YOUR PRAYER LIFE

If you, like many of us, have recognized that your prayer life is not where it ought to be, then there is no need to be disheartened or tempted to give up on God. In fact, He sends both help and comfort to us in our time of need through His Word. Your prayer life can be restored, and your faith can be strengthened. Some keys to improving your prayer life are:

- **Be consistent** – This is having regular prayers at various intervals. It can include, but is not limited to, morning and evening/nighttime prayers. Prayers before meals and before driving. Let prayer become a habit. Bear in mind, your prayer doesn't need to be eloquent and long. Just be consistent and allow God to do the rest.

- **Be intentional** – Cultivate a habit of praying with purpose. This focuses on being specific. You will seek God's guidance and direction in everything that you do—not just opening a one-sided channel, but also paying keen attention to His responses and trying as best as possible to align yourself with His will and purpose for your life.

- **Talk to Him as to a Friend** - In prayer, do not be afraid to open your heart to Christ as to a friend. Tell Him your joys, sorrows, pain, dreams, and aspirations. Interestingly, a few years ago, when I thought about this, I found it very hard because I have a hard time trusting others. I hardly have friends I can truly open up to wholeheartedly, so much so that a friend of mine mentioned something to me one day, and after offering a bit of insight and encouragement, she said, *"Thanks for always being there for me, but when you are always there for others, who listens to you? Who is there for you?"* The quickest response I could give was to jokingly say "God." After I thought about it, I realized there was some truth in that. So the statement, "talk to God as to a friend," coupled with the one that says there is a friend that sticketh closer than a brother, had renewed meaning. Oh, sure, I do have friends and even family members I can really talk to. In fact, having someone to talk to can be very therapeutic, and let's face it, we all need someone to lean on. But look at it this way, when you open up to this friend, there is never any fear that what you mentioned will come back to haunt you.

- **Pray with and for others** - Praying with and for others can enhance our prayer lives. As **"Iron sharpeneth iron; so a man sharpeneth the countenance of his friend." (Proverbs 27:17 - KJV).** I often hear my mother and my older sister say that sometimes, while interceding on behalf of others, they forget their own problems or pain. As a child growing up, I spent my formative years with my aunt in St. Elizabeth and with cousins I consider my brothers and sisters. We learned the power of praying with and for others because our parents prayed. My "daddy" was a leader in the church, and we were known as "Pastor's children." He was always interceding on behalf of others until the day of his passing in September of 2015.

Relocating back to St. Ann to live with my biological parents and siblings was pretty much a continuation of the same. So I have always been a part of a household that prays.

I have often heard Christians say that even when we feel unworthy, we should just pray. I can admit, and I know others will agree, that this is not as simple as it seems.

First of all, whenever I have said or done anything that is contrary to what I know to be morally correct, I find it one of the hardest things to "face God." I feel like it doesn't make any sense to pray, and to add to that, if I go to church and I am asked to participate in service, I politely decline as I sort through the conflicting emotions that are wreaking havoc on the physical man. Some of these battles served to convince me that the devil uses our tests and trials as a means to break us and shatter our faith in Christ.

Doubt and distraction will always be two of the main weapons of the devil. When the devil causes us to feel so broken, he will ensure that we feel as if not even God can help us. He uses our brokenness to cast doubt on the credibility of Christ to keep His promises to us. When Christ says, *He will never leave nor forsake you*, you can hold Him to it. When He says *He will provide*, you can hold Him to it. When He says He will be your comfort, your shelter, and protector, you can take Him at His Word.

When we doubt the power of God and the power of prayer, and we become so distracted that we do not even find or make the time to unlock heaven's portals through faith and our prayers, then the devil knows he has gained some foothold in your life. Wreaking the rest of the havoc he plans to unleash upon your life will be made easier for him.

CHAPTER 8

WHITE COLLAR CRIMINAL

Throughout my life, I have always heard about white-collar and blue-collar crimes. Research has shown that white- collar crimes often involve nonviolent financial offenses, for example, fraud and embezzlement, in contrast to blue-collar crimes, which are typically street crimes like theft and assault. Professional individuals often commit white-collar crimes for their own selfish advantage. In contrast, the latter is committed by persons from lower socioeconomic backgrounds who may use street crime and violence as defense mechanisms or as a means of survival.

To convict both sets of individuals, an investigation will need to be conducted, involving complex financial analysis and forensic accounting. But for the other, they are sometimes easily identified by eyewitnesses and other hard evidence.

Now, based on my analysis, I have concluded that the old serpent, the devil, is a white-collar criminal. This conclusion was based on an investigation that can be conducted using the Bible. Genesis 3:1 portrays him as subtil. It says, **"Now the serpent was more subtil**

than any beast of the field which the Lord God had made." (KJV). This word "subtil" is a variant of the word "subtle." This portrays the devil as being very cunning, crafty, and sly. So, similar to white-collar criminals, we may not be able to readily identify just how he will come at us.

We have been admonished in Ephesians 6:11 to put on the whole armor of God that we may be able to stand against the wiles of the devil. His wiles include any form of cunningness and trickery that will help him accomplish his goals. He has plans to harm us, to entrap us with his lies, deception, discouragement, and snares. His aim is to discourage and confuse us to the point where what is wrong begins to seem right, and what is right seems wrong in some cases. Our consciences will become so seared that we no longer feel guilty about disobeying God, and we become convinced that we can rationalize all our decisions, so even others will believe that our wrongs are actually right, and that is exactly what the devil wants.

He will try his utmost best to highlight the pleasures of sin and present them in some attractive packages that seem so delightful, enticing, and irresistible. But what he will not do is to highlight the consequences or the outcome of indulging in those sinful habits. All sin brings is shame and disgrace, and the looming possibility of being separated from our heavenly Father. But let me remind you that things are not always as they seem. His

Tested and Tried

campaign strategies are enticing and an invitation to treat, and we can not always see clearly the disaster or disappointment that lies ahead.

I will liken this to an experience I had a few years ago. One of my cousins discovered this place on the internet and convinced a few other family members and close friends to join us on a trip. When the pictures were circulated, we all had a chance to look at the vivid and beautiful images and views of nature, which piqued our interest. As a result, the trip was planned, promoted, and soon became a reality.

When we got to the location, we kept looking at our phones at the pictures, trying to make a link with where we were, because we were in utter disbelief that this could be the same place. Some of us had even done our research by asking family members and friends who lived in that area, and no one had ever heard of such an attraction in that specific location. But still we went, thinking they were mistaken, only to be greeted by great disappointment. It was just a river, where some people collected an entry fee and basically left us on our own. Another busload of people arrived, and upon realizing they had been misled by a fake advertisement, they decided to leave immediately.

As it is with us today, the devil lures us into his snares with false advertisement. He will present attractive packages, and when those packages are opened or revealed, we realize that they are not as promising as they seemed. The ads we saw were pleasing to the eyes, but what was the end result? Great disappointment.

Additionally, we would have learnt a few more lessons that day. Firstly, the other group realized that things weren't as advertised, so they left. We stayed, thinking that since we traveled such a long distance, we should make the best of the situation.

Sometimes, when we find ourselves in the devil's trap, we may think that it is the end and that there is no hope for us to break free. But you can choose to leave that situation that has you bound. It won't be easy—that much I know. The devil will not give up without a fight. He will present all the reasons why you would be better off staying where you are.

Secondly, staying almost had detrimental effects. There was this one guy who stayed to be our "guide." He took us further upstream through some bushes to a better part of the river, and some time after, it started to rain. We recognized that he began to get a bit anxious, so by mere curiosity, we tried to get some answers. We were told that the area was prone to lightning strikes and that we were at risk of even losing our lives. At this point, he wasn't even concerned about our safety. Based on previous experiences he had witnessed or heard about, and since he was from the area, his only aim was to get himself out of danger and reach safety. When we considered the

Tested and Tried

possibilities, I, for one, thought, *"I will not die here."* That gave more urgency to our steps. We all started to rush, trying to keep up with him, and saying I was scared would be an understatement because I panicked big time.

So it is with that white collar criminal, the devil. He will lead us down paths of destruction. He knows paths that can be detrimental and even deadly to us. We could have left or should have left with that other busload of people that came, but we chose to enjoy the little pleasures we could get, even though it was already a disappointment. Well, the pleasures of sin will cause you to become stuck in some places and situations that could have been avoided had we been obedient to the voice of the Lord.

When you are brought out of a situation, learn the lesson taught by the experience, avoid making the same mistakes, and share your experience so others do not fall into the same situation.

After experiencing being led to that location by false advertising and the lightning scare, we concluded that, although it was not a completely bad day, we could never be caught at that location again. We had learnt our lesson. We also felt the need to share our experience with others so they wouldn't make the same mistake we did.

God will bring you out of situations you had no business being in the first place. Not only will He bring you out, but He will not hold it against you. In fact, He is willing to give you full restoration. When He does all that for you and more, it is imperative that we help others evade the destructive path the devil waits to lure them onto, as many times, not everyone is as lucky or has the time to make it back to safety.

The devil does go about as a roaring lion seeking whom he may devour. Not only is he a roaring lion, but he is also a white-collar criminal. His schemes and his charm are subtle, and he is a crafty and hateful foe. But just remain steadfast in prayer and the Word of God because His doom is sure. The roaring lion will be defeated once and for all by the Conquering Lion.

CHAPTER 9

BREAKING CHAINS

A few years ago, I was tasked with teaching the young people at church sign language. After going through the alphabet and a few other preliminary words with them, I decided it was time to go to songs. The first song we did was *"There is power in the name of Jesus, to break every chain."* I fell in love with this rendition because there is such profound truth found in the words of that song.

Our Father in heaven wields the only power that can break every chain you encounter in your life. Sometimes the chains that hold us bound are often chains of circumstance that we got ourselves into in the first place. We find ourselves in jobs we have no business being in, in relationships we have no business being in, and living lives we should not be living.

There is a saying: *We create our own storms, then we panic when it starts to rain.* But let's face it, we are guilty as charged, guilty for both binding ourselves by certain circumstances and guilty also of not doing what it takes to break free. The good thing about God, though, is that

He will bring us out of the situations we get ourselves into, and He will not hold it against us.

But conditions apply; we must first be willing to acknowledge that where we are is not where we are to be, reach out to Christ in repentance, and accept His forgiveness. His grace is sufficient for you and for me.

We will all be faced with our fair share of trials. We all have our own crosses to bear. Sometimes the burdens will get so heavy that it seems pointless and hopeless to even pray. But might I remind you that Christ is our burden-bearer.

> **Then they cried unto the Lord in their trouble, and He saved them out of their distresses. He brought them out of darkness and the shadow of death, and brake their bands in sunder. (Psalm 107:13-14 – KJV).**

These verses highlight the fact that as long as you cry out to the Lord in your times of distress, times of sorrow, and times of despair, you will be saved out of them. He is capable, willing, and able to bring you out of darkness and break those bands that hold you captive. Bands in this context are things that restrain or bind. So, in other words, those chains will be broken and you will be free. Christ does not rescue us based on who we are, but because it is in His nature to rescue His children; His very nature is love.

Tested and Tried

As for me, I strongly detest any form of restraint, and I will forever embrace and cherish freedom. In fact, this was one of the facts that a few individuals chose to present to me when I yearned for marriage and companionship. I was told that I would be giving up my freedom and that I should enjoy it while it lasts, along with other comments that made it appear as if wishing for marriage was to be likened to having both hands bound by chains that could only be loosed by the partner at any given time. What surprised me most of all was that the majority of this counsel came from Christian couples. To be honest, I often got so upset whenever I found myself engaged in conversations of this nature. Luckily, I had good and godly examples displayed, especially through my church family and, more so, my family members. Having waded into the marital waters myself, I have recognized that it is quite the opposite. Marriage is freedom—freedom to love someone unconditionally, freedom to be yourself. In essence, freedom to love and be loved.

Freedom in Christ is even more fulfilling because it is liberation from the power and penalty that sin brings. Once these chains are broken, we can become the man or woman Christ intended us to be. You will clearly discover, embrace, and walk into your God-given purpose. It will not always be an easy walk, and that is the reality. But He who has granted you your freedom and even paid for it with His blood will see you through to the end. You may be wondering how you can experience this freedom. It is within your reach, just reach out in faith.

Imagine a scene where there is a prisoner in a cell. He is guilty of the crimes that he has been accused of. He awaits his punishment, thinking that as much as he wishes to be granted some form of reprieve, he is deserving of the penalty. Suddenly, there is a shift in judgment, and he receives a lesser punishment than he deserves. Instead of receiving the punishment he deserved, he is told that bail has been posted for him, and he is finally a free man.

The prison guard calls for him to come forth out of the cell, which had held him captive for a while, yet still he sits there and doesn't move a muscle. The first thing that comes to mind is that he must be crazy, right? He had become so accustomed to his captivity that the thought of being free no longer held the same appeal. Or maybe, to him, the thought of this freedom seemed too good to be true.

Well, what if I were to tell you that the prisoner represents us and our lives on many occasions? Christ has offered us that freedom, yet we refuse to accept it. Our prison doors are wide open, yet we are still sitting in the cell—bound by the chains of our circumstances, bound by chains that are often of our own choosing. He has already paid for our freedom; it is now up to us to accept the gift He has given us.

Tested and Tried

Now, let us continue to be guided by our imagination as we go back to the case of the prisoner. Let's imagine him being told by the judge that all he needs to do to repay the price is to become engaged in service to others. For example, community service activities. If he keeps his side of the bargain, then he is completely a free man. We may all be hasty to say that that is a small and simple price to pay for his freedom. Likewise, Christ paid for our freedom, and all He asks is that we be of service to Him and to our fellow men.

In one of my previous relationships, I was involved with someone who did not share my religious beliefs. As much as we had some good days, our inability to see eye to eye on so many issues cast a shadow on our relationship. Why? The only way to be truly happy at times was to compromise the very thoughts and ideologies that I knew to be right.

On many occasions, I got so caught up that the line between right and wrong became a bit blurred. It was becoming so much easier to accept and rationalize my actions, so much so that it began to feel okay to be in the wrong. I was giving up the freedom I had experienced in Christ for fleeting moments of happiness and snippets of what I thought was freedom, but which was merely ephemeral freedom offered by the devil. All of it was but for a moment in time.

How was I able to bounce back?

At the end of that relationship, I could not understand why. Well, actually, I could. A part of me knew it wasn't working out, but I clung to the hope that it would because I did not want another failed relationship. But God had other plans for my life, and I had to trust His divine plan for me. Was the bounce back easy? No, it was not. However, grace made a way for me to come through—a way for me to rekindle my passion for Christ and regain my freedom in Him. This was no easy feat because the devil is real, but so is God. Bouncing back could only be achieved through the power of prayer.

Have you ever found yourself praying through tears and crying through prayer? You may wonder what the difference is. You may have encountered a situation where the initial response was emotional, and as tears flowed, you were driven to your knees, praying and hoping to find solace.

On the other hand, you may simply go to God in prayer and find yourself starting to weep on your knees. I have experienced both, and I can attest that in both situations, my attitude and approach may have been different, but God's love and His grace remained constant.

So, to answer the question of what freedom truly is? We can never truly experience freedom unless we experience freedom in Christ. This is not merely legal or even social freedom, but rather freedom from sin and its penalty—freedom to live and experience love, joy, peace, and

Tested and Tried

fulfilling your God-given purpose; freedom from the fears and apprehension of tomorrow, and from the guilt and condemnation of your past mistakes.

Are you ready to experience such freedom? Your chains can be broken. Are you living contrary to your spiritual and moral principles? Your chains can be broken. Do you want to access the power of prayer in your life and experience God's abundant grace? Your chains need to be broken.

Accept the freedom He so willingly wants to give to you. Extend your faith and be ready and willing to trust Him, even when the road ahead seems rough and uncertain.

> **If the Son therefore shall make you free, ye shall be free indeed. (John 8:36 – KJV).**

CHAPTER 10

EXPERIENCING TRANSFORMATION

Can a leopard change its spots? The answer is a resounding no. There have been many instances where I have heard this statement used to refer to individuals. It is said that just as the spots on a leopard are natural and cannot be changed, the same holds true for a person's character; some things are simply a natural part of them that cannot be altered. Metaphorically speaking, of course, because even though a leopard cannot in fact change its spots, an individual can indeed experience change in their lives.

> **Can the Ethiopian change his skin, or the leopard his spots? Then may ye also do good, that are accustomed to do evil. (Jeremiah 13:23 – KJV).**

We cannot change the fact that we were born in sin and shaped in iniquity (**see Psalm 51:5**). In other words, that fact shows sin to be our skin and our spots, and it is a fact that we cannot change our sinful inclinations by our own accord. We are powerless to accomplish this in any way, shape, or form. We can only experience transformation by the grace of God; we can only access His abundant grace by activating the power of prayer.

The story is told of a certain individual who used to live a promiscuous lifestyle, and when encouraged to make a change and allow Christ to transform her, her response was, *"This is who I am."* That was the only way of life that she knew. There are other individuals who can identify with this young woman, whether male or female. Some people get caught up in lifestyles that may be deemed hereditary. Others fall prey to being branded by the "family curse." Therefore, because the family has a history of negativity attached to their names, other individuals who try to break free are told that they are, or they must be, because their family members are or were. But this does not have to be your reality, and it's not your identity. Your identity is who you are and who you can be in Christ, as long as you are willing to allow Him to perform the work of transformation in your life.

Speaking of identity, many years ago, while in high school, I had a teacher who seemed to dislike me because of how I looked, not because of who I was as an individual. He had an experience with my sister a few years back, and a few weeks after I was assigned to his class, he started looking at me as if trying to make an association with the face. One day, realization dawned on him. This led him to ask me if I was related to a previous student he had a few years earlier. I told him that the person he was describing was my sister, and it seemed he had a light bulb moment. From then on, as soon as he came to class, he asked me to leave. If he gave an assignment and other students in the class did not do it for various reasons, he would ask us all to stand and still ask me to leave the class. I allowed this on a few occasions because I may not have been feeling in the mood for class on those days. However, one day I decided that I had had enough and I took a stand. Needless to say, that was the end of that phase, and things returned to normal.

Likewise, you may be suffering the effects of being identified with your family. It may not even be something bad on the part of your family, but how it is seen or perceived by others. As with my sister's case, she did not do anything wrong or disrespectful in the eyes of others, but the teacher had a different point of view and allowed it to fester, ultimately affecting another generation. But at some point or another, you have to take a stand and reclaim your life. The enemy wants you to bow and admit defeat, but you can still be victorious. All hope is not lost. You can have a new identity in Christ.

You are not defined by who society says you are or even by what others think about you. You are defined by who Christ says you are and who He created you to be.

IDENTITY CRISIS

Research indicates that an identity crisis involves intense self-reflection and questioning about one's sense of self, purpose, and place in the world. Have you ever found yourself going through such a crisis? If you answered yes, I want to remind you that you are not alone. In fact, it is a natural part of life and is often very prevalent during changes, especially in young people transitioning into adulthood. We are at times so confused that we allow others to define who we are and even who we should be. We get so caught up in trying to live up to the expectations of others that we lose our very identity.

A friend of mine visited the office some time ago, and as we got to talking, he expressed that he was stressed. However, he hastened to point out that our generation knows how to deal with it. He also expressed his concern that the "younger generation" does not really know how to effectively manage stress. To which I agree somewhat. Our young people today are influenced by the identities they see on social media, and they confuse reality with what they see. They will try to adapt to and follow those highlights of "happiness," often unaware that some of these people project fake images that have captivated their minds and clouded their vision. Sadly, the line between illusions and reality becomes so blurred that some lose their lives, some, their sight of the true meaning of life, and consequently, their identity and purpose.

However, contrary to what others would have you think, there is no situation that is too hopeless. Prayer is a powerful tool that can unlock any chain. It will also help to dispel the forces of darkness and bring light to dark situations.

As my brother always says to us, pray daily, minutely. He encouraged us to make regular deposits to the prayer bank, and at times, he reminded us that sometimes it is not even the prayers that we have prayed or even the ones that we are praying that is being answered at any given moment in time, but the prayers that have been deposited in the prayer account by our friends, family members or even other random individuals who remain prayerful on our behalf, even without our knowledge.

So, even when you do not feel like praying, pray. Even if you don't consider yourself able to pray, talk to God. He will hear and understand even the groanings that are uttered.

> **Likewise the Spirit also helpeth our infirmities: for we know not what we should pray for as we ought: but the Spirit itself maketh intercession for us with groanings which cannot be uttered. And he that searcheth the hearts knoweth what is the mind of the Spirit, because he maketh intercession for the saints according to the will of God. (Romans 8:26-27 – KJV).**

As a Christian, I have had many moments when I felt so unworthy to talk to God, but I was encouraged to pray anyhow. While you do not have to be a Christian to talk to this Supreme being, you do need to develop a relationship with Him.

It is comforting, however, to know that no matter what comes, regardless of what our lives are like now or even what your prayer life is like, you can experience transformation. But God will not force this transformation on you. This is a matter of choice. You and I must choose to make time for prayer. Be intentional about your prayer life and allow prayer to become a lifestyle and a habit. Be as open to Him as with a friend. Let Him be the central focus of every decision that you make in your life. He is waiting with eyes, ears, and arms wide open.

We must also make a choice not to allow doubt, distractions, and discouragement to rob us of the joy we can experience as long as we remain prayerful and grounded in Him. He calls us to a life of repentance, and He promises us complete restoration.

We will also experience transformation when we let go and let God. Let your faith be bigger and stronger than your fear. I recently read that faith is not just about everything turning out okay; more importantly, it is about being okay, no matter how things turn out. This shows explicit trust in God and choosing Him over and over in the midst of challenging and overwhelming situations. Even though we will get fearful, as is the human response to problems, faith tells us to trust. Let your faith be stronger than your fear.

CONCLUSION/MOMENTS OF REFLECTION

In moments of quiet reflection, I have realized that accessing the power of prayer is not a simple task. The reality is that our prayer lives lack depth or connection to the one true God.

Prayer often becomes ritualistic and is used only as a spare tyre, not as the engine that powers our lives. Until prayer becomes the "engine," we will not gain access to its true power.

The good thing about it, though, is that there is hope. There is hope for you and for me. If, like me, you have discovered that your prayer life is not what it ought to be, then make it your priority to draw closer to God and deepen that relational bond with Him. It is then and only then that you will truly understand that His "yes, no, and wait" are for your own good, and you will be able to be at peace with whatever the outcome is.

This relationship will not only improve the quality of your life but also strengthen you to deal with the crucibles that come your way. Additionally, you will learn to access and unlock the incredible power of prayer and bask in God's abundant grace.

Remember to keep praying.

> **"Pray without ceasing." (1 Thessalonians 5:17 – KJV).**

POEMS

FROM THE AUTHOR

TESTED AND TRIED

We have all been tested and tried
But never had to fight on our own.
For some, only God knows the tears we've cried
But we were never left alone.

You may have gone through your season of pain
If not, brace yourself, it's coming.
And remember, there is not always sunshine immediately after the rain
You just have to learn to trust God's timing.

You may feel that there is not much more you can take
But just hold on a little longer.
These tests and trials are not meant for you to break
They come to make you stronger.

THE POWER OF PRAYER

Prayer is a very powerful weapon
Believe it or not, it's true.
More powerful than weapons of mortal man
Just pray and watch God come through for you.

Many are yet to access its true power
Because without faith, it is impossible.
Talk with God every minute, every hour
And even the impossibilities will become possible.

It is important to feast on His Word like daily food
Just seek to know Him even better.
You will understand that yes, no, or not yet is for your own good
And let Him have His way in the matter.

GRACE

God gives us His unmerited favour
That is His abundant grace.
We are broken creatures in need of a Saviour
To help us run this tedious race.

He loves you with an everlasting love
His grace is sufficient for you.
Our one true God who reigns in heaven above
Just trust Him, remain faithful, and to Him be true.

ABOUT THE AUTHOR

Sanola Rose Lawrence is an author, writer, and aspiring speaker who has been a Christian for nearly her entire life. She has served in various capacities across multiple departments of her church, including Youth & Children's Ministries, Treasury, Deputy Pathfinder Director, and Music Ministries.

Her journey of faith has been marked by numerous accounts of God's goodness to her, and she capitalizes on every opportunity to share the love of God with others through sermons or engaging discussions. She remains committed to the work of the Lord and seeks to develop a deeper and more meaningful relationship with Him.

Born in the garden parish of St. Ann, she spent her formative years in the breadbasket parish of St. Elizabeth. She then relocated to St. Ann during her teenage years, where she has lived ever since.

She is a proud graduate of Ferncourt High School and the Northern Caribbean University and has been employed at Tax Administration Jamaica for the past sixteen years.

Sanola is an aspiring best-selling author and motivational speaker, and she has been happily married for the past three years to Romeo Lawrence, her best friend of almost fifteen years. She is grateful for her strong support system, including her partner, immediate and extended family, friends, and, by extension, her church family.

It is her desire that her work will encourage you to remain faithful to Christ and discover and walk in your purpose.

www.ingramcontent.com/pod-product-compliance
Lightning Source LLC
Chambersburg PA
CBHW070248100426
42743CB00011B/2177